OSCAR'S ARMY

THE SWANSONG OF HITLER'S REICH WAS THE SOUND OF KATYUSHA ROCKETS LANDING ON THE STREETS OF BERLIN IN 1945. THEIR EXPLOSIONS WERE WITNESSED BY A BATTLE WEARY INFANTRY PRIVATE, HIS NAME OSCAR POHL. BUT HE WAS NO ORDINARY FOOTSLOGGER. HE'D SURVIVED POLAND, FRANCE, AND RUSSIA. NOW, BY HOOK OR BY CROOK, HE WAS GOING TO WALK AWAY FROM THIS TOO.

SOMEONE'S GETTING A PASTING.

AS LONG AS IT'S NOT US, I'M HAPPY.

STORY
MIKE KNOWLES

ART
VILA

COVER
IAN KENNEDY

THE GERMAN HAD SPOKEN TOO SOON. THE BARRAGE ENVELOPED THEM AND
WHEN THE SMOKE CLEARED OSCAR WAS ALONE. AS HE CROSSED A STREET,
HE RECITED THE OLD TRAINING TIPS WHICH HAD KEPT HIM ALIVE SO FAR.

WHEN
CROSSING OPEN
SPACES, MOVE
FAST WHILST
ZIGZAGGING.

RIGHT NOW IT WASN'T ARTILLERY OR ROCKETS
HE WAS SCARED OF, IT WAS SNIPERS. LIKE THE
ONE WHOSE SHOTS ONLY JUST MISSED HIM.

PHEW!
THAT WAS LUCKY.
ONCE THOSE KILLERS
GET YOU IN THEIR
SIGHTS, YOU CAN
USUALLY KISS
THE WORLD
GOODBYE.

IT WAS A BITTER BLOW FOR THE TWO MEN HAD GROWN UP TOGETHER IN HAMBURG IN THE SAME STREETS. OSCAR'S ATTITUDE HARDENED FROM THAT DAY ON.

IT JUST SHOWS YOU, PROMOTION AND MEDALS ARE JUST NOT WORTH IT. IT'S GETTING OUT ALIVE THAT COUNTS.

HEARING THE SOUND OF BOOTS, OSCAR MOVED TO THE SHADOWS. A SQUAD OF SOLDIERS MOVED PAST — A SO-CALLED S.S. FLYING COURT-MARTIAL UNIT LOOKING FOR DESERTERS TO EXECUTE ON THE SPOT.

MY PAPERS ARE IN ORDER, BUT I'M TAKING NO CHANCES WITH THESE FANATICS.

AS HE STRAIGHTENED UP TO MOVE ON, A BROKEN CHILD'S TOY TRIGGERED A MORE RECENT MEMORY OF A SMALL ORPHANAGE HE HAD COME ACROSS A FEW DAYS BEFORE.

I DIDN'T HANDLE THAT SITUATION TOO WELL.

THE BUILDING HAD BEEN SITUATED IN THE SUBURBS AND THE CHILDREN WERE HUDDLED IN A LARGE CELLAR.

PLEASE HELP US. THE PEOPLE LOOKING AFTER US RAN AWAY.

I'LL SEE WHAT I CAN DO.

AN ORPHAN HIMSELF, OSCAR HAD HAD TO LIVE ON THE STREETS, LIVING BY HIS WITS. THAT HAD TOUGHENED HIM AND TAUGHT HIM THE ART OF SURVIVAL.

OUTSIDE IN THE DARKNESS OSCAR'S SEARCH FOR HELP BROUGHT HIM TO A TRUCK GUARDED BY A DETACHMENT OF S.S. MEN. DESPITE HIS DISTRUST OF ANYBODY IN THAT UNIFORM, HE APPROACHED THEM FOR ASSISTANCE IN EVACUATING THE ORPHANS TO A SAFER AREA.

NAGAL'S IN CHARGE, BUT YOU WON'T GET ANY JOY FROM HIM.

IT'S WORTH A TRY.

AS PREDICTED, THE S.S. HAUPTSTURMFUHRER DISMISSED OSCAR'S SUGGESTION, HALF-BLINDING HIM WITH A TORCH AS HE DID SO. THE VEHICLE WAS PACKED WITH IMPORTANT FILES WHICH HE INTENDED TO DELIVER.

WHAT? DUMP VITAL DOCUMENTS TO MAKE ROOM FOR A BUNCH OF SCRUFFY ORPHANS?

BUT, SIR . . .

ALTHOUGH HE WOULD NEVER ADMIT IT, OSCAR FELT GUILTY ABOUT DESERTING THOSE ORPHANS. HE PRESSED ON, NOW USING THE SEWERS, MAKING FOR THE FACTORY WHICH WAS HIS UNIT'S RENDEZVOUS POINT.

I WONDER HOW MANY OF MY KAMERADEN MANAGED TO MAKE IT THERE?

BACK ON THE SURFACE HE FOUND THE BUILDING. WORRIED SOME TRIGGER-HAPPY SENTRY MIGHT SHOOT FIRST, OSCAR HID BEHIND A WRECKED TRUCK BEFORE GIVING THE PASSWORD.

WHEAT-BEER . . . NOT THAT THERE'S MUCH OF THAT LEFT NOW.

COME ON IN THEN, OSCAR.

AS USUAL, THE VETERAN'S ARRIVAL WAS GREETED WITH A MIXTURE OF SHEER AWE AND AMUSEMENT BY HIS FELLOW SOLDIERS.

LOOK AT THAT. NOT A SCRATCH ON HIM

HOW DO YOU DO IT, OSCAR?

I'M A BORN SURVIVOR, MATE.

COLONEL LEOPOLD LUTZ AND THE ADJUTANT, CAPTAIN RUDI HERNALS, WERE IN THE BASEMENT, WARMING THEMSELVES BY A STOVE, WHEN HE REPORTED IN.

BUT, SIR . . .

AH, POHL. I'M PROMOTING YOU TO SERGEANT. YOU'RE ONE OF THE MOST EXPERIENCED SOLDIERS WE HAVE.

AS A FURTHER SALVO OF KATYUSHA ROCKETS WENT ON ITS WAY, OSCAR WAS TEMPTED TO PROTEST — UNTIL HE RECALLED A RECENT DIRECTIVE FROM HIGH COMMAND THAT ANY SOLDIER REFUSING TO OBEY AN ORDER WERE TO BE SHOT.

COME WITH ME, SERGEANT.

YOU SAY YOU LACK LEADERSHIP QUALITIES? WELL, YOU'D BETTER FIND SOME FAST BECAUSE YOU'LL BE NEEDING THEM.

JUST AS HE THOUGHT IT COULDN'T GET ANY WORSE, THE WILY INFANTRYMAN FOUND HIMSELF FACING A BUNCH OF WHAT SEEMED LIKE SCHOOLBOYS IN UNIFORM.

SERGEANT POHL, MEET YOUR PLATOON.

I AM SENIOR CADET JOSEF BRAUCHITSCH, SERGEANT.

BUT THESE ARE SAILORS, SIR!

14

THEIR ORDERS WERE SIMPLE. FOR THE GERMAN FORCES, THE DAYS OF COMPLICATED MILITARY TACTICS WERE OVER.

WE'RE TO HOLD OUR POSITION AND STOP THE IVANS ADVANCING.

YOU MAY REST ASSURED WE'LL DEFEND IT TO THE LAST MAN, SERGEANT.

OSCAR RESISTED THE TEMPTATION TO LAUGH AT SUCH POMPOUS TALK. AS HE TURNED AWAY, ONE OF THE LADS, WILLI WEBER, CALLED AFTER HIM.

HAVE YOU ANY ADVICE FOR US, SERGEANT?

FIND SOME COVER AND WAIT. I'M GOING OUT TO SCOUT THE AREA. IN THE MEANTIME, BRAUCHITSCH IS IN CHARGE.

TURNING HIS BACK ON THE ENEMY, HE MADE TO WALK AWAY.

IF THOSE KIDS ARE SO KEEN TO DIE, THEN WHO AM I TO STOP THEM? LOTS OF PEOPLE ARE DYING — YOUNG AND OLD.

HE HAD SEEN TOO MUCH OF IT RECENTLY. BOYS IN UNIFORM SHOT DOWN BEFORE THEY HAD EVEN FIRED A ROUND. A HOME FULL OF AGED INVALIDS BURNING FIERCELY AND NO HOPE OF ESCAPE. BUT SOMETHING NAGGED AT HIS MIND.

MOVING OFF, HE RECALLED HE'D HAD A SIMILAR TWINGE OF CONSCIENCE AT THE ORPHANAGE — AND ALMOST WOUND UP DEAD BECAUSE OF IT.

MORE FOOL THEM FOR TRUSTING ME. ANYONE STUPID ENOUGH TO FALL FOR HITLER'S PROPAGANDA HAS ONLY THEMSELVES TO BLAME.

AND YET HE TURNED BACK.

HE TIMED IT PERFECTLY, STRIKING THE SOFT BELLY OF THE T-34. THE SHAPED HIGH-EXPLOSIVE CHARGE RIPPED THROUGH THE STEEL PLATE.

WE'RE HIT!

THEN, AS THE CREW OF THE NOW-BURNING T-34 BALED OUT, THEY CAME UNDER A HAIL OF BULLETS FROM THE MAKE-SHIFT SQUAD.

URGH!

AAGH!

TRY TO KILL US, WOULD YOU?

TO DEAL WITH THE INFANTRY, OSCAR HAD PLACED THE CADETS IN POSITIONS THAT GAVE THEM THE BEST FIELD OF FIRE. THIS INCLUDED SOME COMMANDED BY BRAUCHITSCH IN AND ON A WRECKED TRAM.

OSCAR TOO PLAYED HIS PART IN THE SKIRMISH, ENCOURAGING THE CADETS, DESPITE HIS EARLIER CYNICISM.

WHEN THE SHOOTING FINALLY STOPPED, ONLY SEVEN OF THE
CADETS REMAINED. BRAUCHITSCH WAS STILL AS INDOCTRINATED
AS EVER AND HIS ATTITUDE MADE OSCAR GROAN INWARDLY.

HEIL HITLER! I REGRET TO REPORT, SERGEANT, THAT THREE OF THE CADETS RAN AWAY.

GOOD FOR THEM. THEY SHOWED SOME SENSE.

AN ANGRY FLUSH CAME OVER SENIOR CADET BRAUCHITSCH'S FACE.

SERGEANT, I MUST PROTEST . . .

NEIN, YOU MUST NOT! IF OUR TOP BRASS HAD ANY SENSE THEY'D SURRENDER. AND STOP ANY MORE OF THIS USELESS BLOODSHED.

BRAUCHITSCH WAS FULL OF NAZI FERVOUR, ASSUMING HIS FELLOWS TO BE THE SAME. TO HIS DISGUST ONLY TWO CADETS CHOSE TO REMAIN WITH HIM, ALL THE OTHERS SIDING WITH OSCAR.

DON'T WORRY. WE'LL NOTIFY YOUR NEXT OF KIN THAT YOU DIED A HERO'S DEATH.

WHAT CAN THREE OF US DO?

AS THE VETERAN AND HIS CHARGES MADE THEIR WAY THROUGH THE CITY, THEY HEARD THE SOUND OF KATYUSHA ROCKETS LANDING IN THE DISTANCE. WEBER PASSED ON NEWS TO THEIR SERGEANT WHO DID NOT HIDE HIS GRIN.

BRAUCHITSCH AND HIS FRIENDS HAVE DECIDED TO SEE SENSE, SERGEANT, AND ARE FOLLOWING US.

I THOUGHT THEY MIGHT. IT'S ALMOST DARK, SO WE'D BETTER FIND A PLACE TO REST.

THAT NIGHT, HOLED UP IN THE CELLAR OF A BOMB-DAMAGED HOUSE, OSCAR WAS ENCOURAGED TO TELL THE CADETS STORIES OF HIS PAST CAMPAIGNS IN POLAND AND FRANCE AND RUSSIA. HE AGREED RELUCTANTLY.

IN NINETEEN-THIRTY-NINE WE ALL HOPED FOR A QUICK WAR. FAT CHANCE OF THAT.

SO YOU WERE FIGHTING FROM THE VERY START?

WEBER'S WORDS BROUGHT A RESPONSE FROM BRAUCHITSCH WHO HAD RECOVERED HIS ARROGANCE QUICKLY.

HOW CAN A SOLDIER WHO FOUGHT IN POLAND, FRANCE AND RUSSIA STILL HAVE BEEN A PRIVATE AND ONLY PROMOTED YESTERDAY?

OSCAR GRINNED AT BRAUCHITSCH WHO LOOKED ANGRY.

SOME ARE BORN TO LEAD, OTHERS ARE BORN TO FOLLOW.

SIGHING DEEPLY, OSCAR DECIDED TO SHARE HIS OPINION ON MILITARY PROMOTION.

A SOLDIER'S GOT ENOUGH PROBLEMS LOOKING AFTER HIS OWN SKIN, LET ALONE OTHER PEOPLE'S. KEEP YOUR HEAD DOWN AND LET SOME OTHER FOOL VOLUNTEER — THAT'S MY MOTTO.

BUT SURELY YOU MUST HAVE HAD SOME AMBITION?

AN UNEASY SILENCE FOLLOWED AND THE CADETS GOT WHAT SLEEP THEY COULD. IN THE EARLY HOURS OF THE MORNING, THE CADET ON WATCH, JOACHIM HILDEBRANDT, WAS SURPRISED TO SEE BRAUCHITSCH AND HIS TWO CRONIES MOVE TO SLIP AWAY.

WHERE ARE YOU GOING?

WE'RE NOT STAYING WITH THAT COWARD AND TRAITOR. ARE YOU COMING WITH US, HILDEBRANDT?

THE BESPECTACLED CADET SHOOK HIS HEAD DEFIANTLY.

I WAS ORDERED TO GUARD MY COMRADES AND I WON'T LET THEM DOWN.

VERY WELL, HAVE IT YOUR OWN WAY.

LATER OSCAR TOOK THE NEWS OF THE DESERTIONS CALMLY BUT WEBER WASN'T SO SURE. HE KNEW THE NAZI OF OLD.

GOOD RIDDANCE TO THEM. I HATE MOANERS.

I KNOW BRAUCHITSCH, SERGEANT. HE'LL REPORT US IF HE GETS A CHANCE.

THE ANSWER CAME WHEN A BUILDING COLLAPSED, RAISING A HUGE CLOUD OF DUST AND PROVIDING A SORT OF SMOKE SCREEN.

HERE'S OUR CHANCE. RUN FOR IT.

BUT WE COULD BE HEADING STRAIGHT INTO THE IVANS.

GRITTING HIS TEETH IN DETERMINATION, BRAUCHITSCH CLAMBERED OVER THE RUBBLE AND RAN AS FAST AS HE COULD.

IN THAT CASE WE'LL DIE FOR THE FUHRER.

PAUSING BETWEEN MOUNDS OF
RUBBLE, OSCAR APPLIED A FIELD
DRESSING TO WEBER'S ARM.

YOU'RE LUCKY, IT'S JUST A GASH. I'VE SEEN SHRAPNEL TAKE AN ARM OFF.

CAN YOU TEACH US TO IDENTIFY ARTILLERY, SERGEANT? WE WANT TO BE EXPERTS LIKE YOU.

OSCAR'S REACTION WAS
TO BURST OUT LAUGHING.

IT TAKES YEARS . . . AND WE DON'T HAVE TIME. I'M TAKING YOU LOT TO A FLAK TOWER.

WHAT FOR, SERGEANT?

ONCE AGAIN THIS HARDENED VETERAN HAD FELT HIS CONSCIENCE STIRRING. THE FLAK TOWER — A MASSIVE ANTI-AIRCRAFT POSITION — WAS VIRTUALLY BOMB AND ARTILLERY PROOF.

YOU CAN SIT OUT THE WAR IN SAFETY THERE. NOW COME ON. WE HAVEN'T GOT ALL DAY.

BUT STILL THE LADS HESITATED.

NOW WHAT?

WE SWORE AN OATH TO SERVE THE FUHRER, SERGEANT. AND HE'S ORDERED US TO FIGHT.

THAT'S RIGHT.

THERE WAS NO POINT IN STAYING SO OSCAR SHEPHERDED HIS CHARGES OUTSIDE. AS THEY LEFT, THE ARTILLERYMAN ADDED ONE MORE DETAIL TO THE STORY.

BY THE WAY, THERE WERE THREE NAVAL CADETS LIKE YOU WITH THE FANATICS.

BRAUCHITSCH AND HIS PALS, I BET.

JA. AND THAT MEANS THE S.S. WILL BE LOOKING FOR US TOO.

NOW THE FUGITIVES HAD TO AVOID CONTACT WITH A ROGUE S.S. UNIT AS WELL AS THE SOVIET SHOCK TROOPS WHO WERE GAINING GROUND INCH BY BLOOD-SOAKED INCH.

THERE'S HEAVY FIGHTING OVER THERE, SERGEANT.

IN THAT CASE WE'LL MAKE A LITTLE DETOUR.

AS THEY MOVED OUT, THE CADETS LOOKED WORRIED AT THE TASK THEY HAD BEEN ASSIGNED.

IT CAME FROM THE SOUTH WEST. TRY THAT WAY.

OSCAR'S SELF-PRESERVATION STRATEGY KICKED IN AGAIN . . .

WHAT DO WE DO?

DON'T WORRY. THE MAN'S SHELL-SHOCKED AND I'VE NO INTENTION OF DESTROYING ANY IVAN GUN . . . UNLESS IT THREATENS US.

. . . THEN HE HAD A CHANGE OF MIND. SUDDENLY HE KNEW THAT IT WAS TIME TO MOUNT A MISSION AND CARRY OUT A DARING RAID. HE TURNED TO HIS "ARMY".

ON THE OTHER HAND, MAYBE IT'S TIME WE DID CAPTURE SOMETHING. THIS IS GOING TO SOUND CRAZY, BUT THEN EVERYTHING IS CRAZY AT THE MOMENT . . .

THE SHEER CHEEK OF IT ALL TOOK THE CADETS' BREATH AWAY. OSCAR WAS PLANNING TO FIND AND ATTACK THE S.S. AND RENEGADE CADET SQUAD, STEAL BACK THE FOOD THEY HAD TAKEN THEN USE IT TO FEED THE ORPHANS HE HAD COME ACROSS EARLIER.

THE PLAN WAS UNLIKELY TO WORK, THOUGH, AS NAGAL'S COMBINED FORCE OF S.S. AND NAVAL CADETS WAS RUNNING OUT OF LUCK. A SOVIET HALF-TRACK PATROL CAUGHT THEM AS THEY MOVED FROM ONE STRONGHOLD TO ANOTHER. GUNS BLAZED.

AS OSCAR FILLED HIS WATER BOTTLE, HE LOOKED AT THE YOUNGSTERS AND SHOOK HIS HEAD IN AMUSEMENT.

THANKS TO YOUR PAL BRAUCHITSCH, THOSE FELLOW GERMANS ARE OUT TO KILL US. THEY DON'T WORRY THAT THEY'RE OUR COUNTRYMEN.

JA, THE SERGEANT'S RIGHT. WE HAVE TO GET THEM FIRST.

WELL, IF YOU PUT IT LIKE THAT.

WITH THAT DECIDED, OSCAR CONTINUED, GRIMLY.

OUR FIRST JOB IS TO INCREASE OUR FIREPOWER. THAT'LL MAKE UP FOR YOUR LACK OF EXPERIENCE AND GIVE US AN EDGE, I HOPE.

AS NIGHT FELL THEY STOLE OUT TO SCOUR THE BATTLEFIELD FOR DISCARDED WEAPONS. AS DAWN BROKE HE EXAMINED THEIR HAUL.

THAT M.G.-THIRTY-FOUR MACHINE GUN SHOULD CAUSE SOME DAMAGE.

AND WE FOUND THESE TWO ASSAULT RIFLES TOO, SERGEANT.

OSCAR WAS PLEASED. THE MP44 ASSAULT RIFLE, CAPABLE OF FIRING UP TO SIX HUNDRED ROUNDS PER MINUTE, WAS MORE ACCURATE THAN THE PPSh SUB-MACHINE GUN THEY HAD ALSO BROUGHT. A GOOD MIX, HE THOUGHT.

WELL DONE. NOW WE CAN GET DOWN TO BUSINESS.

WE'RE LISTENING . . .

THEIR BEST CHANCE WAS TO FIND THIS S.S. UNIT BEFORE THEY FOUND THEM. HILDEBRANDT TOOK OSCAR'S BINOCULARS AND LOOKED FOR A VANTAGE POINT.

KEEP YOUR EYES PEELED FOR THE HALF-TRACK THEY STOLE. AND KEEP YOUR HEAD DOWN.

THEY WATCHED AS HILDEBRANDT CLIMBED UP THE REMAINS OF A SHATTERED BLOCK OF FLATS TO GAIN SOME HEIGHT FOR A BETTER VIEW.

HE'S LIKE A MONKEY.

HE WAS ALWAYS THE FIRST UP THE MAST.

FROM A HIGHER FLOOR, THE LAD COULD SEE OVER THE WAR-TORN CITY.

THE SERGEANT WAS RIGHT. THE WAR IS LOST. I JUST HOPE MY PARENTS ARE . . .

AS HE PEERED OUT THERE CAME THE CRACK OF A RIFLE, AND THE YOUNG CADET DIED. IT WAS A TARGET NO SNIPER COULD HAVE RESISTED.

UGGHH!

THE SHOCKED CADETS LOOKED AT THEIR FALLEN COMRADE THEN AT OSCAR. HE SHRUGGED, HIS FACE IMPASSIVE.

THOSE WERE A GOOD PAIR OF ZEISS BINOCULARS. I TOOK 'EM FROM AN OFFICER.

AND HILDEBRANDT?

ALTHOUGH OSCAR WASN'T SHOWING IT, HE BLAMED HIMSELF FOR HILDEBRANDT'S DEATH.

HIS LUCK RAN OUT.

TO THE SURPRISE OF THE OTHERS, OSCAR TURNED TO WEBER WITH A LOOK OF TRIUMPH IN HIS EYE.

YES, IT'S A PITY HE COULDN'T SMELL THE ENEMY LIKE YOU, SERGEANT.

THAT'S IT! THEY'LL PROBABLY WAIT UNTIL DARK, AND THEN WE CAN FIND THEM!

WHAT, SERGEANT? YOU'VE LOST ME . . .

FOR A MOMENT THE CADETS WERE PUZZLED, THEN THE SOLUTION DAWNED ON THEM.

DON'T YOU SEE? THEY STOLE THE TRUCK AND FOOD.

SO THEY'LL BE HAVING A FEAST! WE'LL BE ABLE TO SMELL IT.

THAT'S IT, LAD.

OSCAR, MG34 IN HAND, WENT ON AHEAD TO SCOUT AND TRY TO DETERMINE IF THEY WERE ON THE RIGHT TRACK.

I HOPE THOSE LADS ARE UP TO THIS. HERE'S ME GOING LOOKING FOR TROUBLE! STILL, NEEDS MUST.

AN HOUR LATER HE RETURNED TO THE ANXIOUSLY WAITING CADETS.

WAS IT THEM, SERGEANT?

YES, THEY'RE IN A BASEMENT. WE'LL GIVE THEM TIME TO RELAX BEFORE WE STRIKE.

THE THREE CADETS WHO HAD SIDED WITH THE S.S. HAD EATEN, THEN BEEN SENT OUT TO KEEP GUARD. THE GOOD FEED HAD MADE THEM DROWSY, BUT THAT CHANGED WHEN A FIGURE APPEARED FROM THE RUBBLE.

MEIN GOTT, IT'S WEBER! WHAT ARE YOU DOING HERE?

I'VE DECIDED TO COME AND JOIN YOU . . .

WEBER HAD JUST BEEN THE DECOY, THOUGH. NEXT SECOND, LIKE A GHOST FROM THE SHADOWS, OSCAR MADE HIS MOVE.

DROP THOSE RIFLES! AND NO HEROICS!

THE STEELY GAZE ABOVE THE MG34 BROOKED NO ARGUMENT.

THE DUEL RAGED ON. NAGAL HAD EDGED TOWARDS A WAY OUT AND WAS ABOUT TO MAKE A RUN FOR IT WHEN A STICK GRENADE SAILED IN CLOSE TO HIM.

MEIN GOTT . . . GOT TO GET CLEAR!

AS HE RAN, THE BLAST OF THE EXPLODING GRENADE TORE AT NAGAL'S CLOTHES, BUT THE REAL DANGER LAY AHEAD OF HIM . . . WHERE OSCAR WAS WAITING.

AAGH!

THIS HAS GONE ON LONG ENOUGH!

THE MG34 ROARED. IT WAS OVER.

WHEN ALL WAS QUIET AGAIN,
THE CADETS BROUGHT IN
THEIR PRISONERS.

WHAT ABOUT THESE THREE?

LET THEM GO. WE DON'T MURDER PEOPLE LIKE THE S.S.

THOUGH OSCAR MAY HAVE THOUGHT THIS WAS THE END OF THE MATTER, FATE HAD ONE MORE SURPRISE IN STORE FOR THEM. A RUMBLING EXPLOSION SIGNALLED A HIT ON THE BUILDING BY A SOVIET KATYUSHA ROCKET. DUST AND MASONRY BEGAN TO FALL.

WHAT THE DEVIL?

THE ROOF'S GOING! RUN FOR IT!

64

LIKE MANY OTHERS ALONG THE WAY, WEBER HAD UNDERESTIMATED OSCAR'S INCREDIBLE KNACK FOR SURVIVAL. HE HAD BEEN BURIED IN A POCKET OF AIR AMONGST THE RUBBLE AND HAD SOMEHOW DUG HIMSELF OUT. BADLY BRUISED, BUT NOT SERIOUSLY HURT, HE HAD DECIDED ENOUGH WAS ENOUGH AND HE, TOO, HEADED FOR THE AMERICAN LINES.

IT'S ALL OVER, PAL. YOUR FUHRER IS DEAD.

HE WASN'T MY FUHRER. ANYWAY, HE SHOULD HAVE STUCK TO BEING A CORPORAL. THEY MADE ME A SERGEANT, AND THE WORLD FELL IN ON ME . . .

Commando
THE END

ON SALE NOW!

No. 4108 £1.25 **Commando**
FOR ACTION AND ADVENTURE

CASTAWAY SQUADRON

No. 4109 £1.25 **Commando**
FOR ACTION AND ADVENTURE

SPLIT-SECOND TIMING

No. 4110 £1.25 **Commando**
FOR ACTION AND ADVENTURE

DEATH DUEL

www.commandomag.com

CONTACT DETAILS By post: The Commando, D.C. Thomson & Co., Ltd, 2 Albert Square Dundee DD1 9QJ
email: editor@commandomag.com
phone: **01382 223131**

PROMOTIONS promotions@dcthomson.co.uk
SUBSCRIPTIONS subscriptions@dcthomson.co.uk
SYNDICATION syndication@dcthomson.co.uk
CIRCULATION circulation@dcthomson.co.uk

COMPETITION RULES Employees of D.C Thomson and their families are not eligible for prizes. The Editor's decision is final and no correspondence will be entered into.

ADVERTISING SALES
email: robin@o20.co.uk
020 7321 0701
or
01372 802 300

LICENSING
start.licensing@btinternet.com

♻ **recycle**
When you have finished with
this magazine please recycle it.

Printed and Published in Great Britain by D.C. Thomson & Co., Ltd., 185 Fleet Street, London EC4A 2HS.
© D.C. Thomson & Co., Ltd., 2008